When You Give A Seed

Written by: Lauren Candies Tarpley   Illustration by: Alvin Cadiz

When You Give A Student A Seed

Copyright © 2024 by Lauren Candies Tarpley

All rights reserved

No portion of this book may be reproduced, stored in a retrieval system, or transmitted in any form by any means-electronic, mechanical, photocopy, recording, or other-except for brief quotations in printed reviews, without prior permission of the author.

Second Edition

Paperback: 979-8-33341-098-6

For my children, who inspire me to create meaningful stories while embracing a purposeful life, and for my husband, who has motivated me and shared every moment of this journey with me.

Love, Mom!

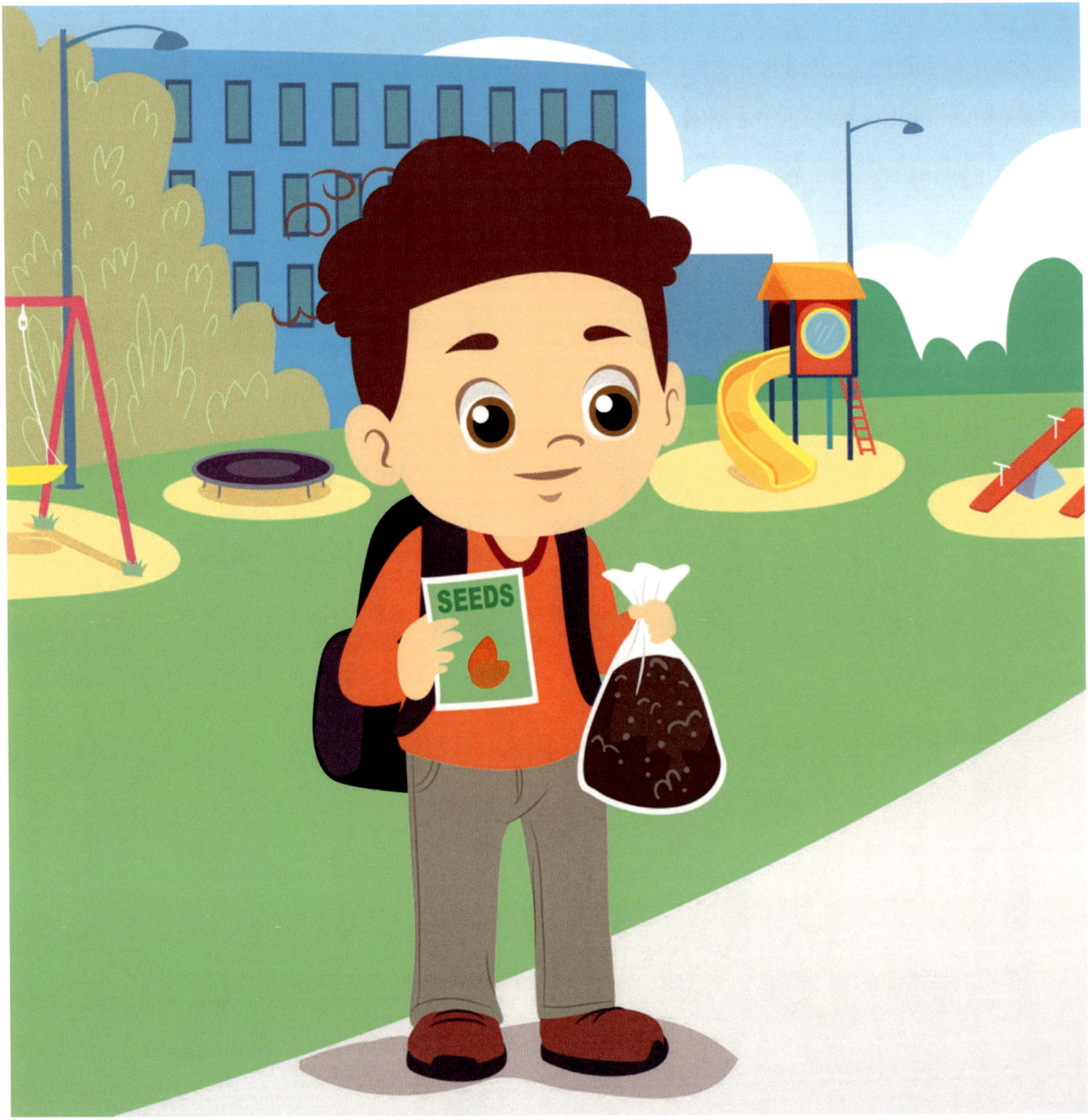
SEEDS

When you give a student a seed, they'll need a special place to plant it.
They will also need some soil to get started.

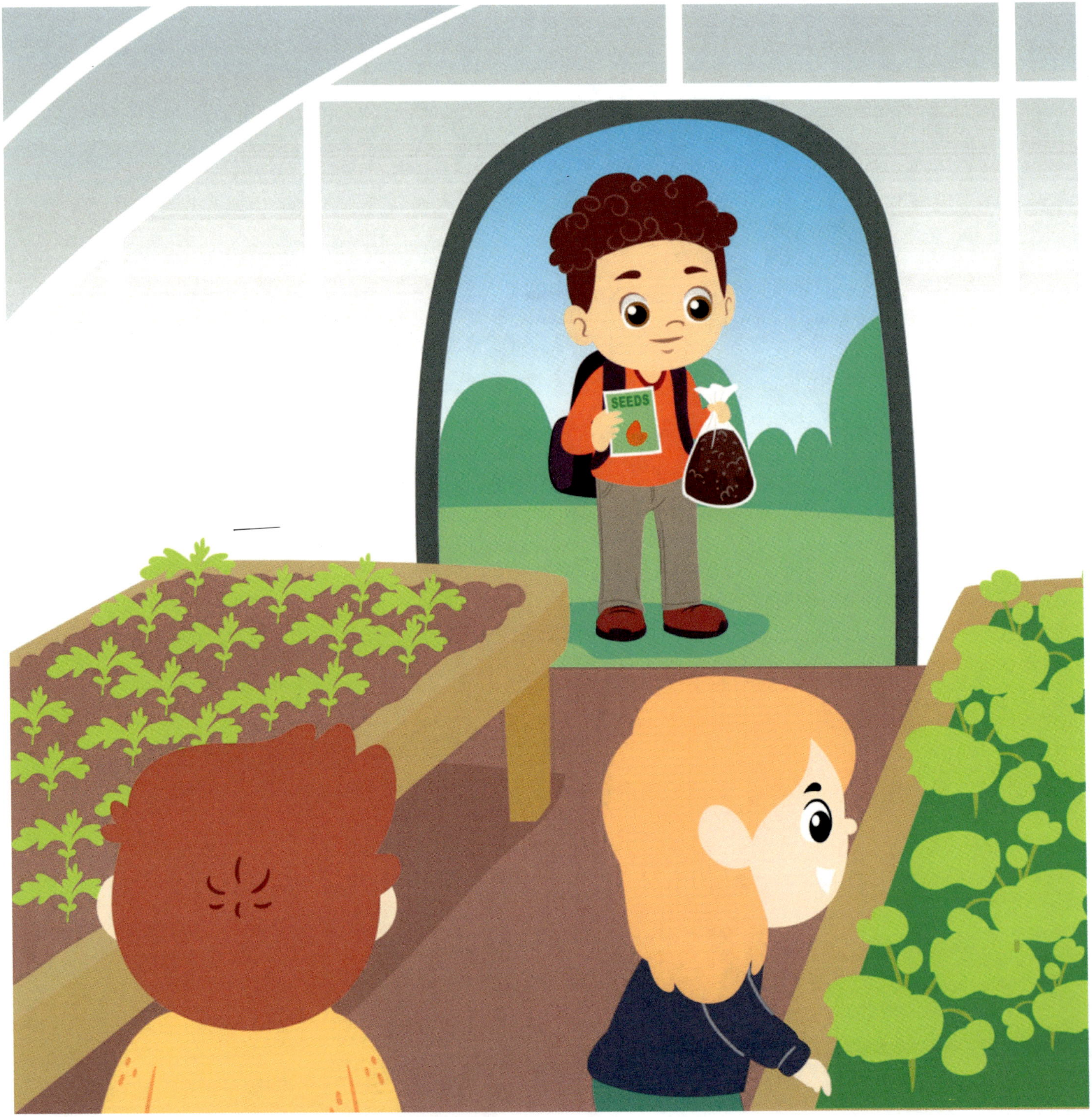
SEEDS

As they search for the perfect spot with the best soil, they'll discover many neat things. There are a lot of great places to plant their seed.

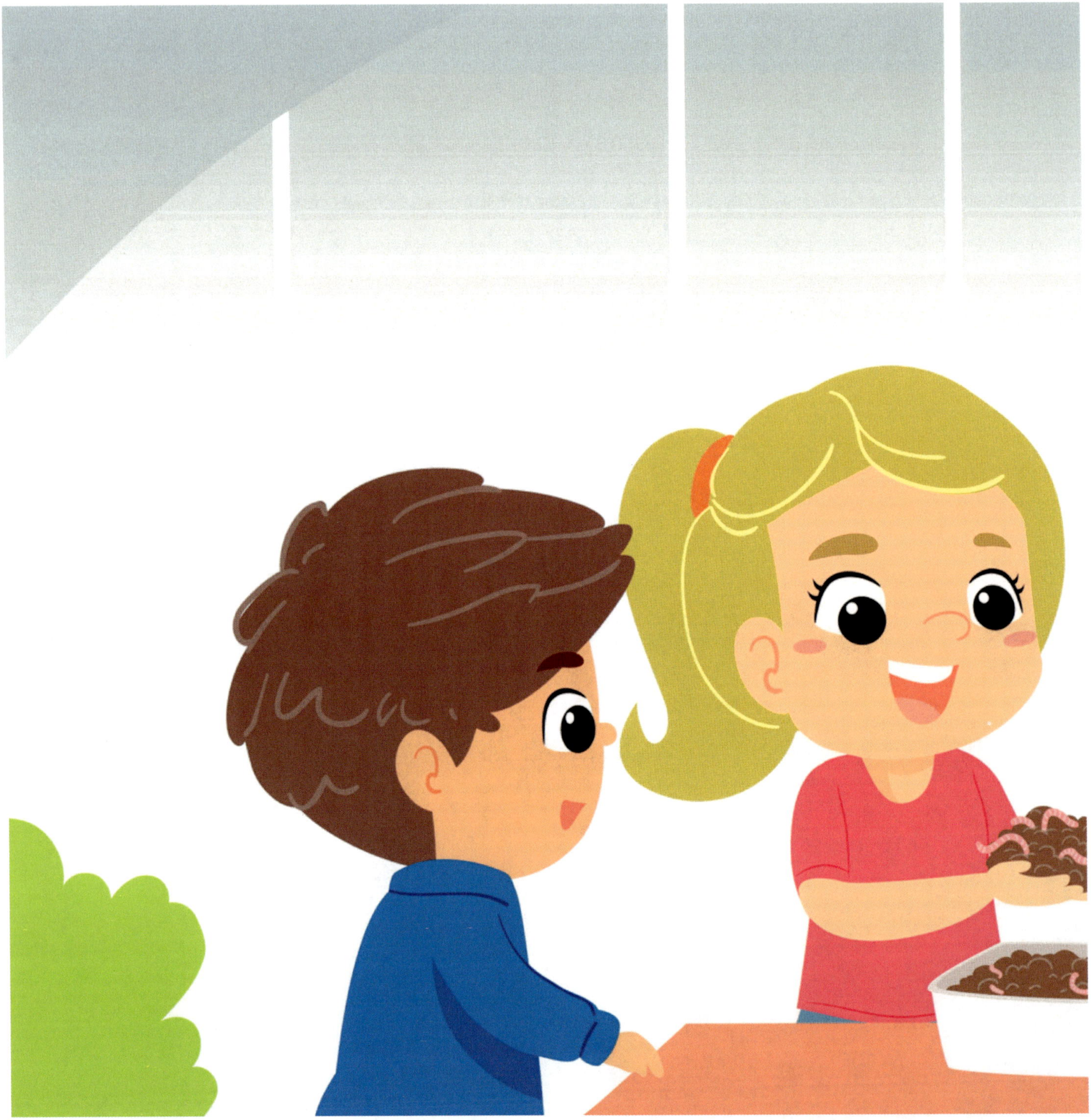

Along their quest, they learn how earthworms are crucial for healthy soil.
They take special care of the worms in the worm garden in their classroom

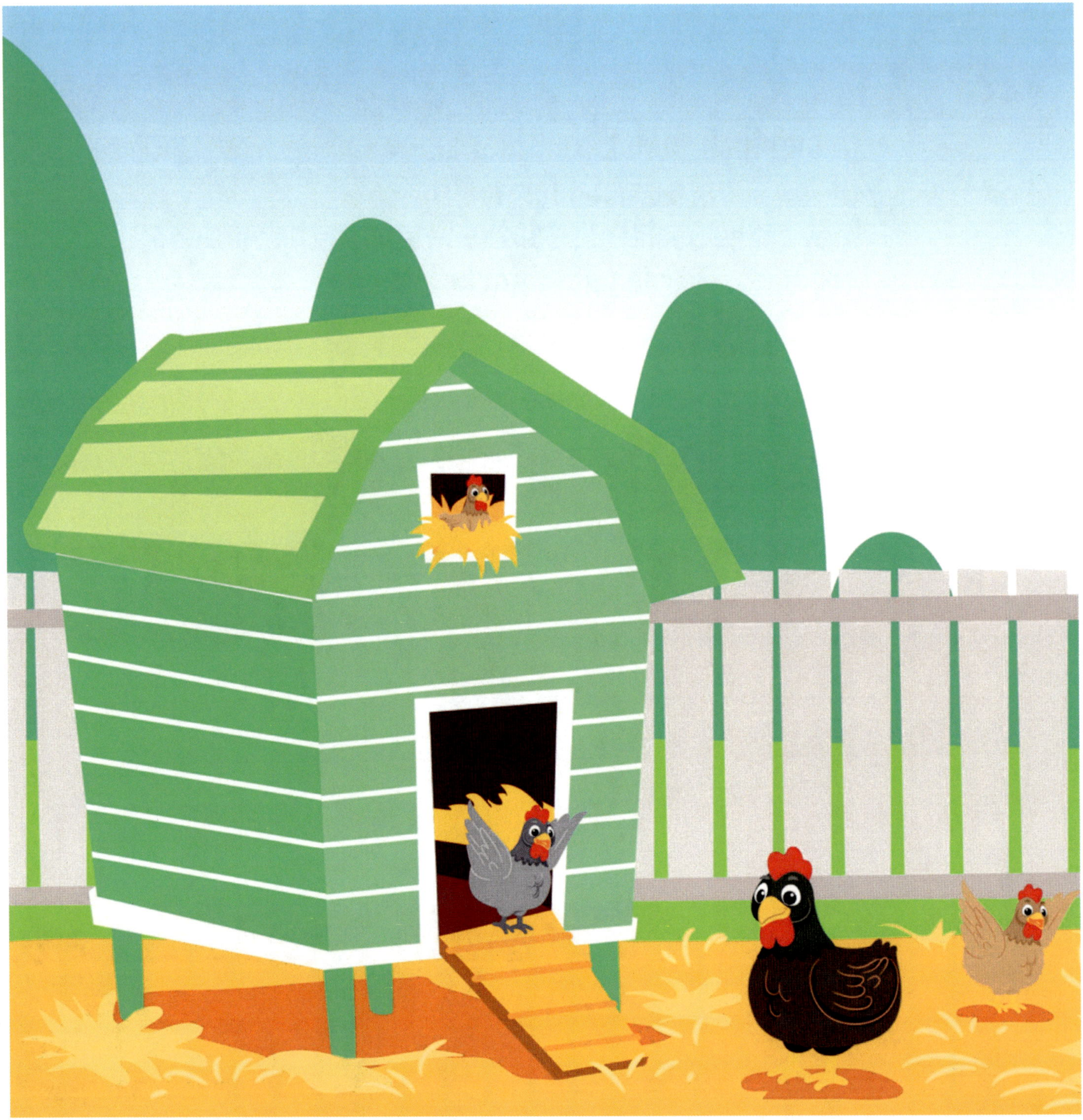

While they search for the best spot,
they'll stumble upon the chicken coop.

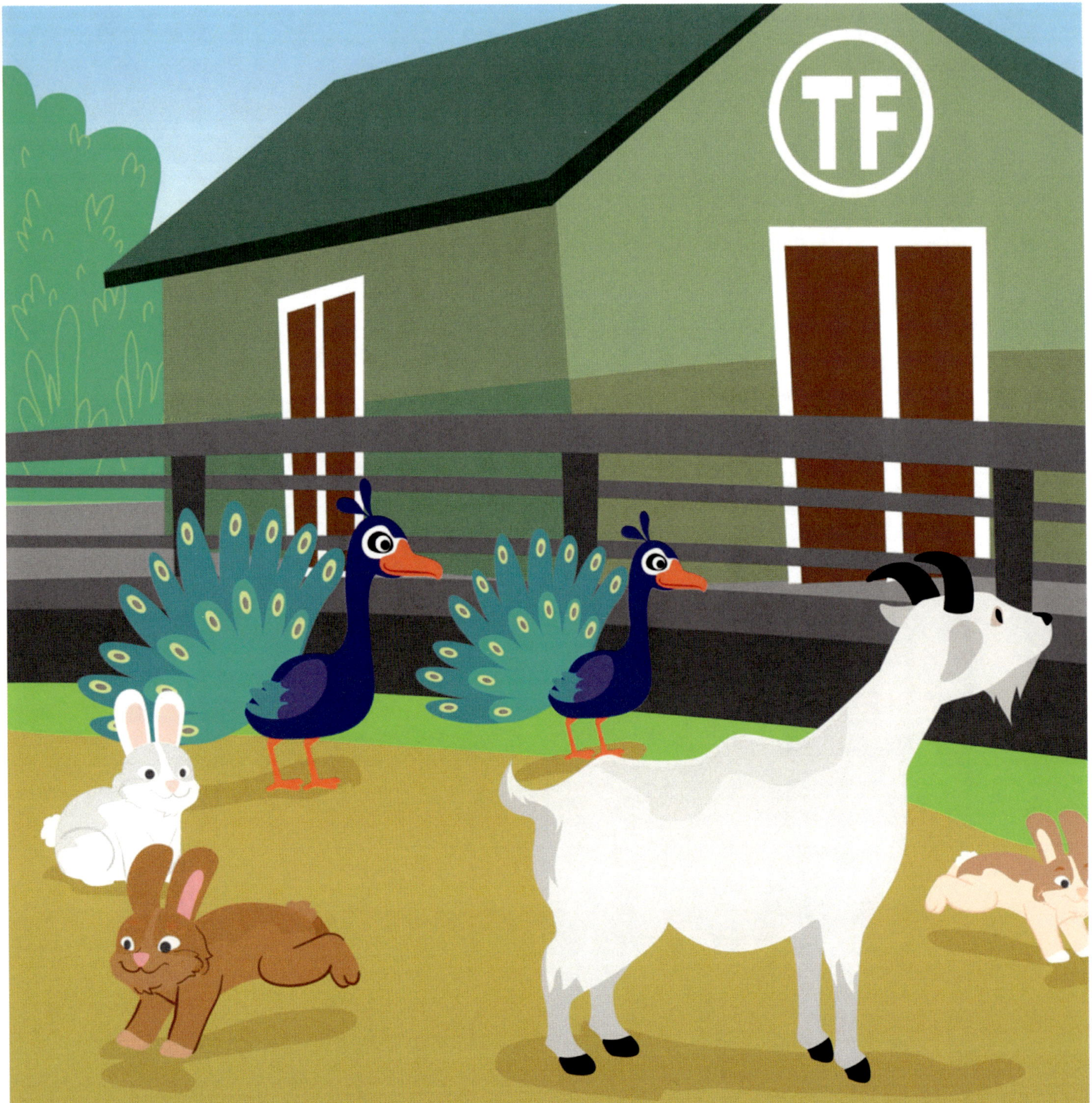
TF

When they visit the chickens, they can't help but meet the other animals on the school campus, too.

After planting their seed, they'll want to water it just right; not too little, not too much!

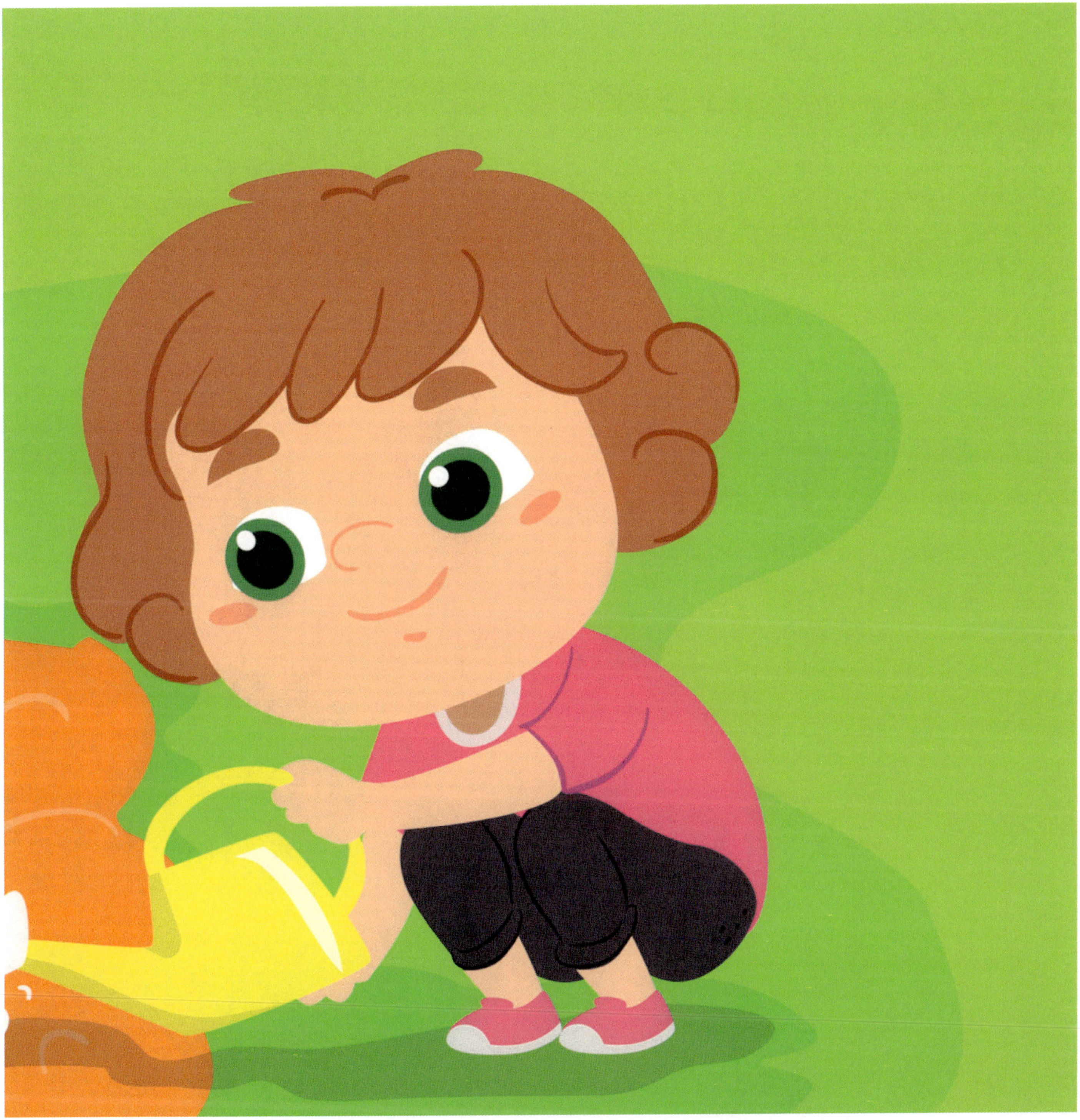

Sometimes, as the students go to water their plants, it might start to rain, and they'll learn all about weather!

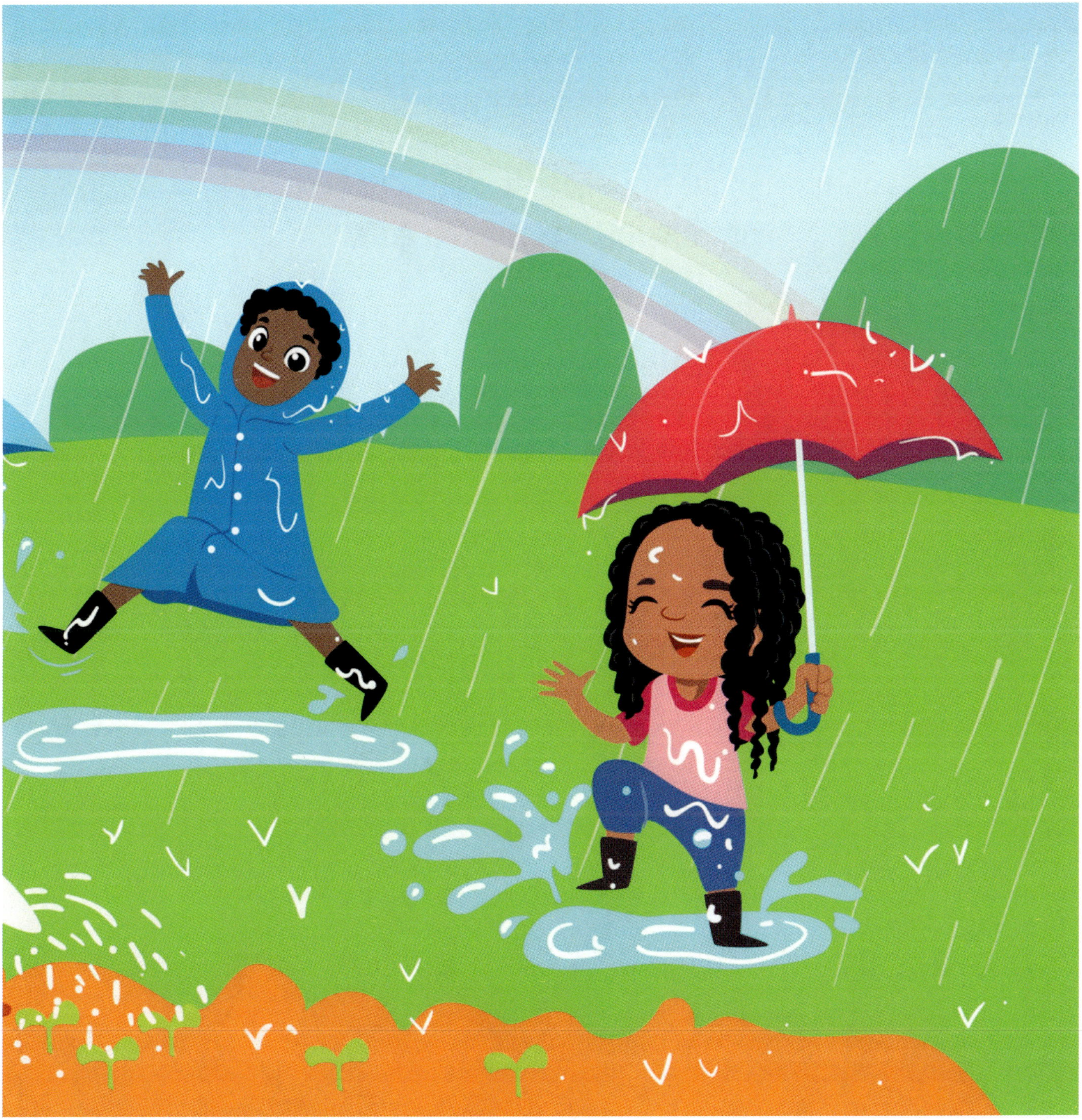

Learning about the weather, they'll understand how it helps their plants grow.

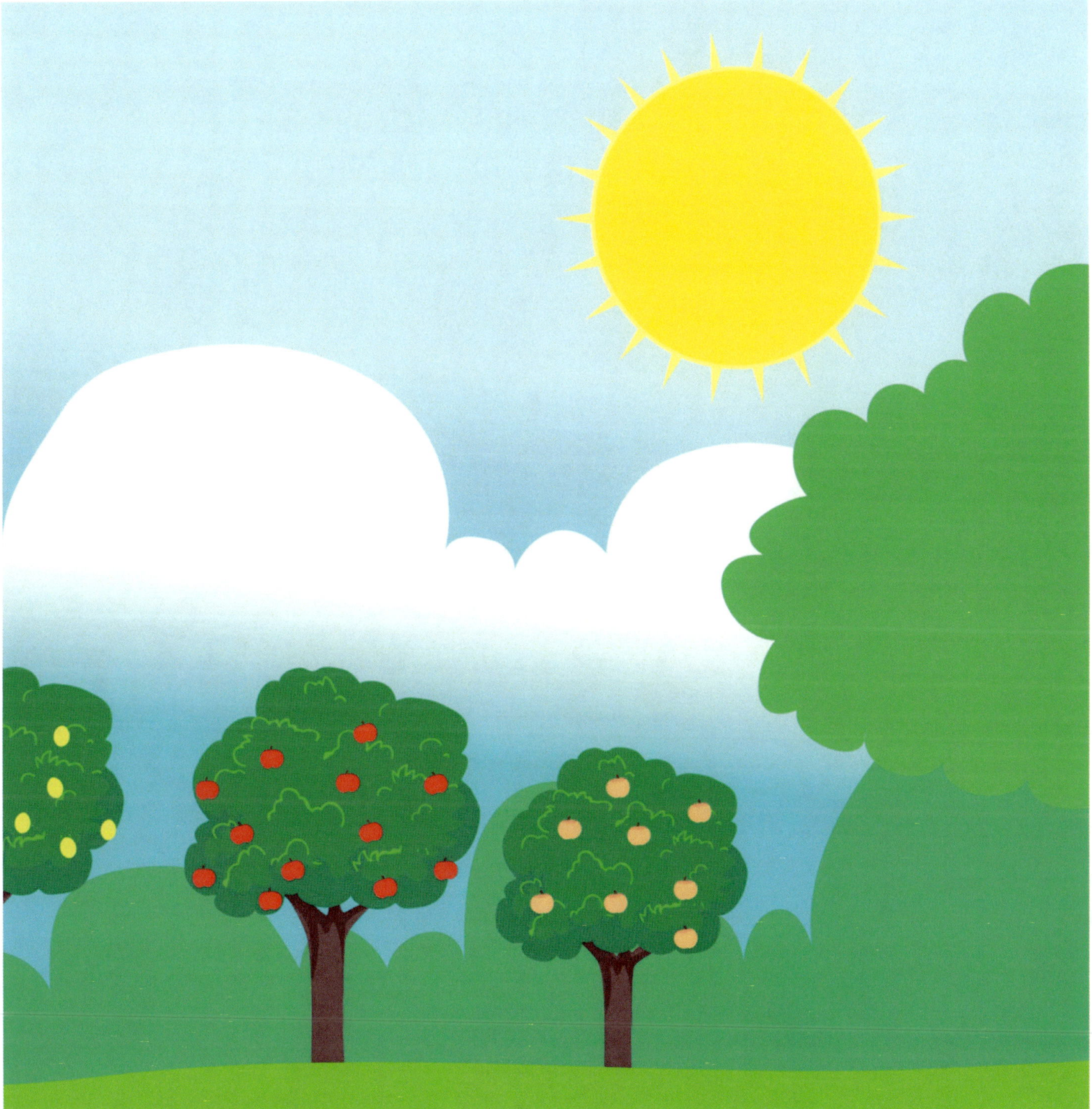

They must be patient and watch as their plants slowly rise from the soil.

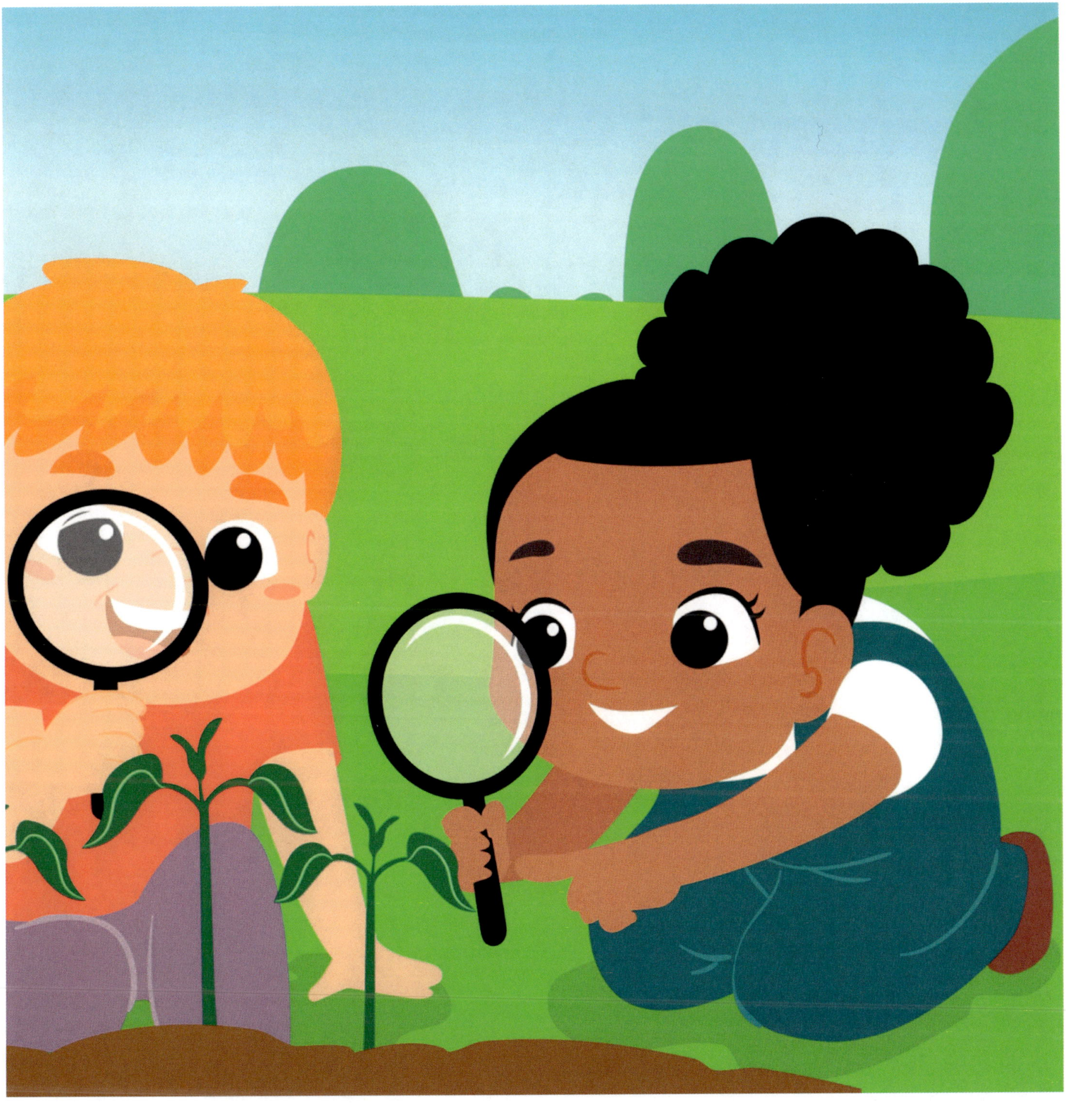

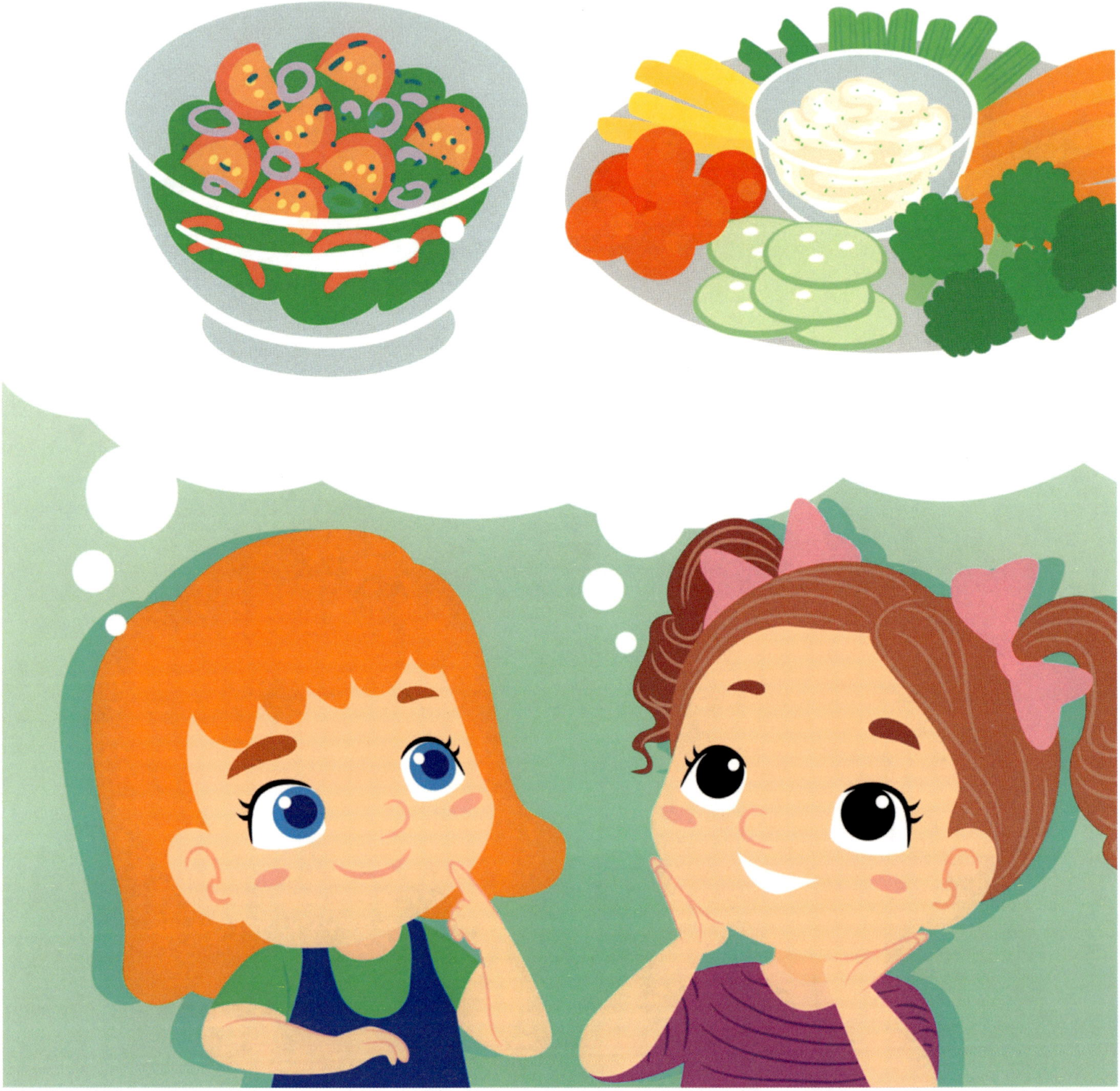

As they watch their plants grow, they'll start imagining all the tasty dishes they could make. They'll think of new recipes and different foods they could try at home and with friends.

As they recap their day with their family, they excitedly tell them all about the amazing things they grew at school. Soon, they're all in the kitchen, cooking together with ingredients from their own garden!

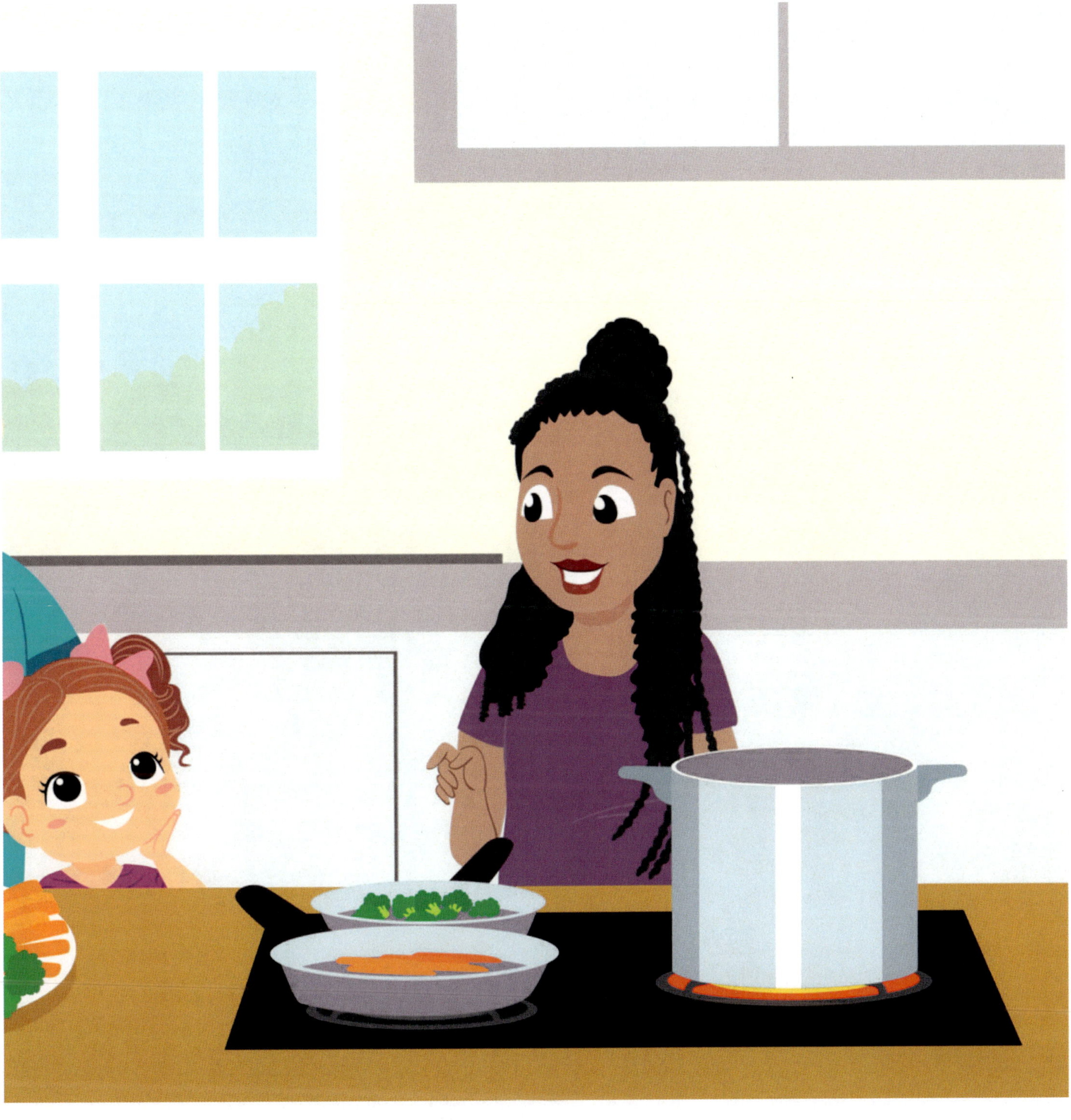

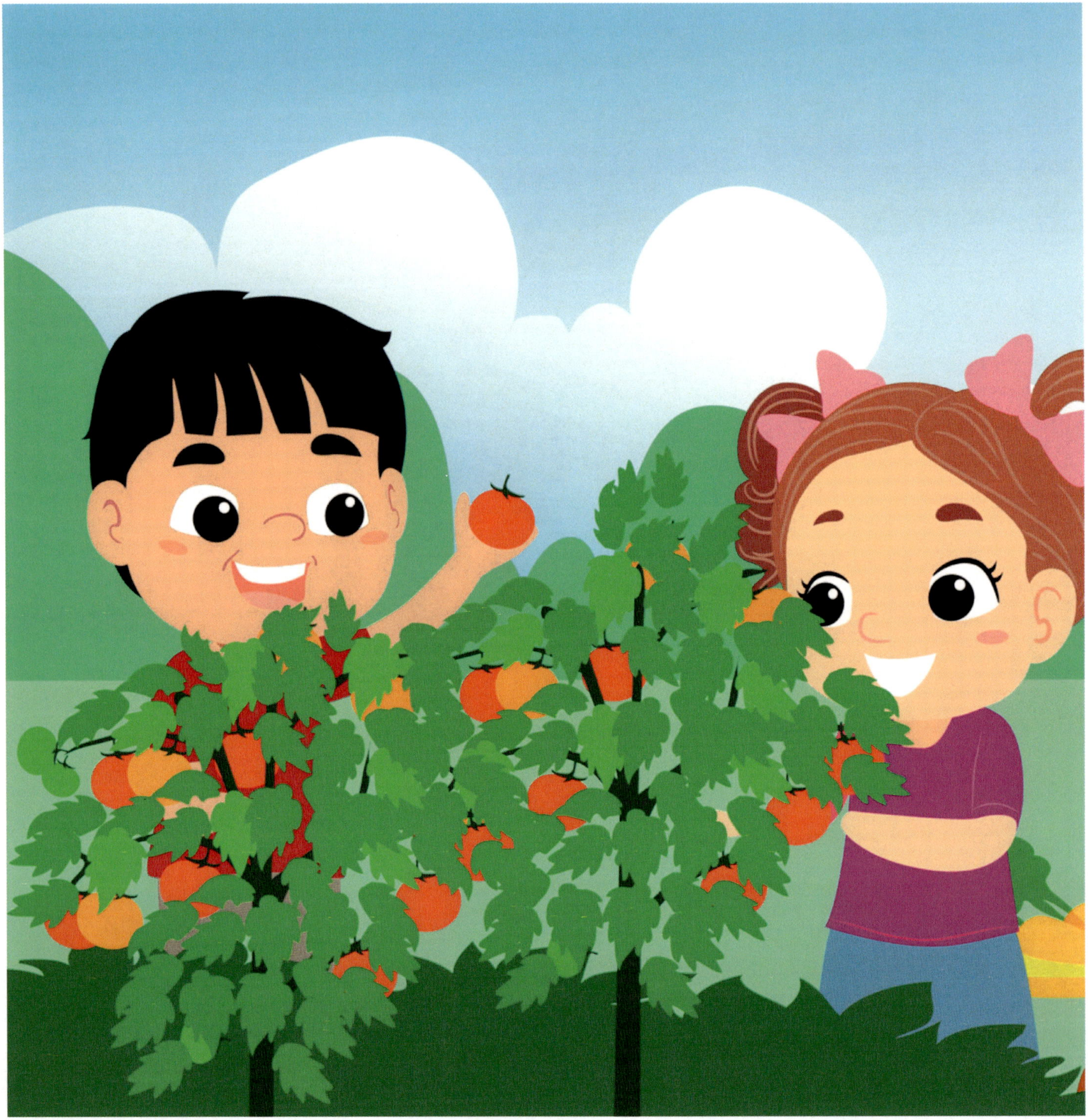

When harvest time arrives, they'll pick their veggies and prepare to cook what they've grown.
But cooking leads to scraps...

They'll take these scraps to school and learn about the importance of composting.

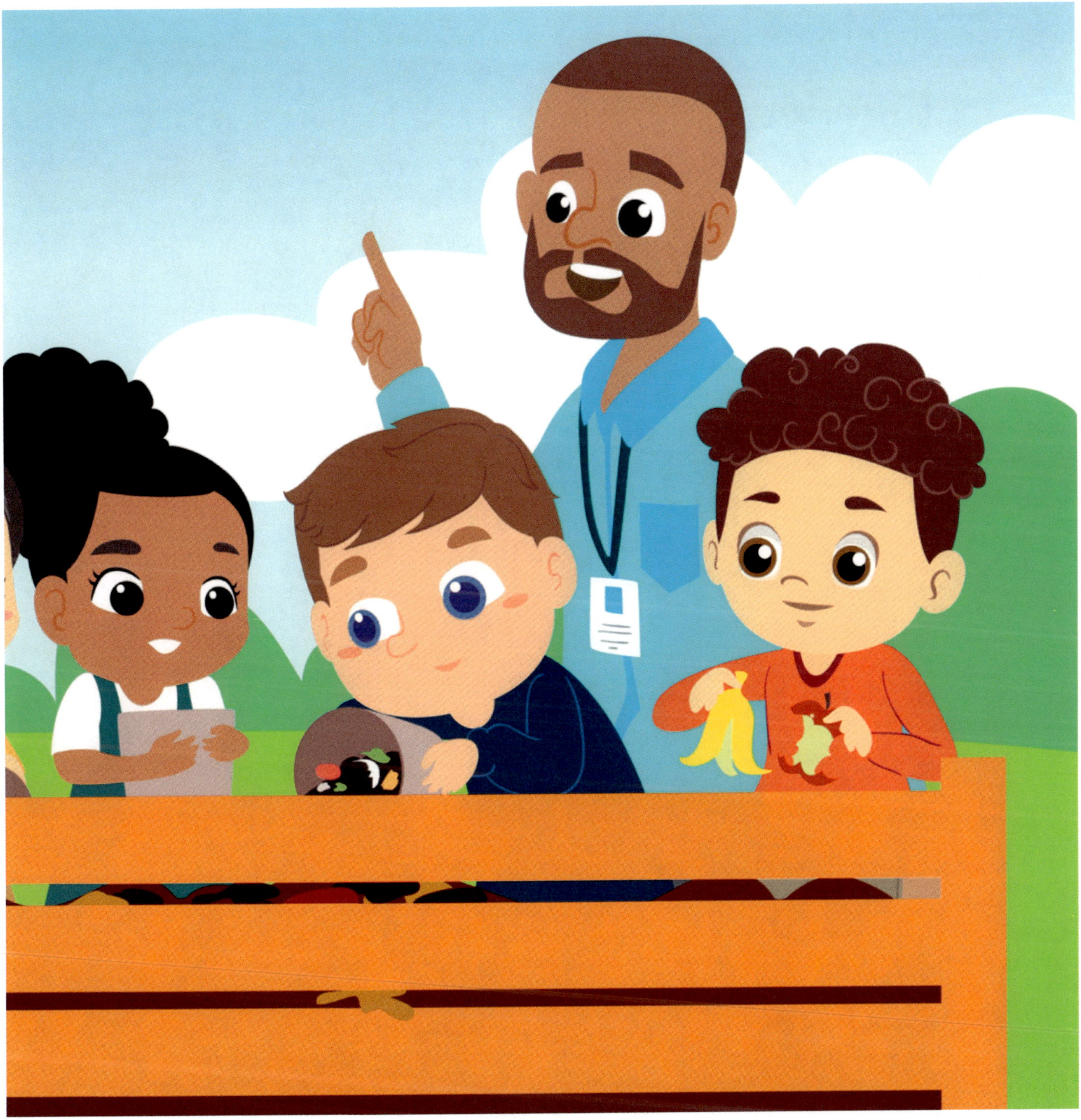

While bringing scraps to the compost area, they notice the school's garden buzzing with activity. The garden is being pollinated! They see many different pollinators. Hummingbirds, dragonflies, birds, and especially bees help the plants grow by moving pollen between the plants.

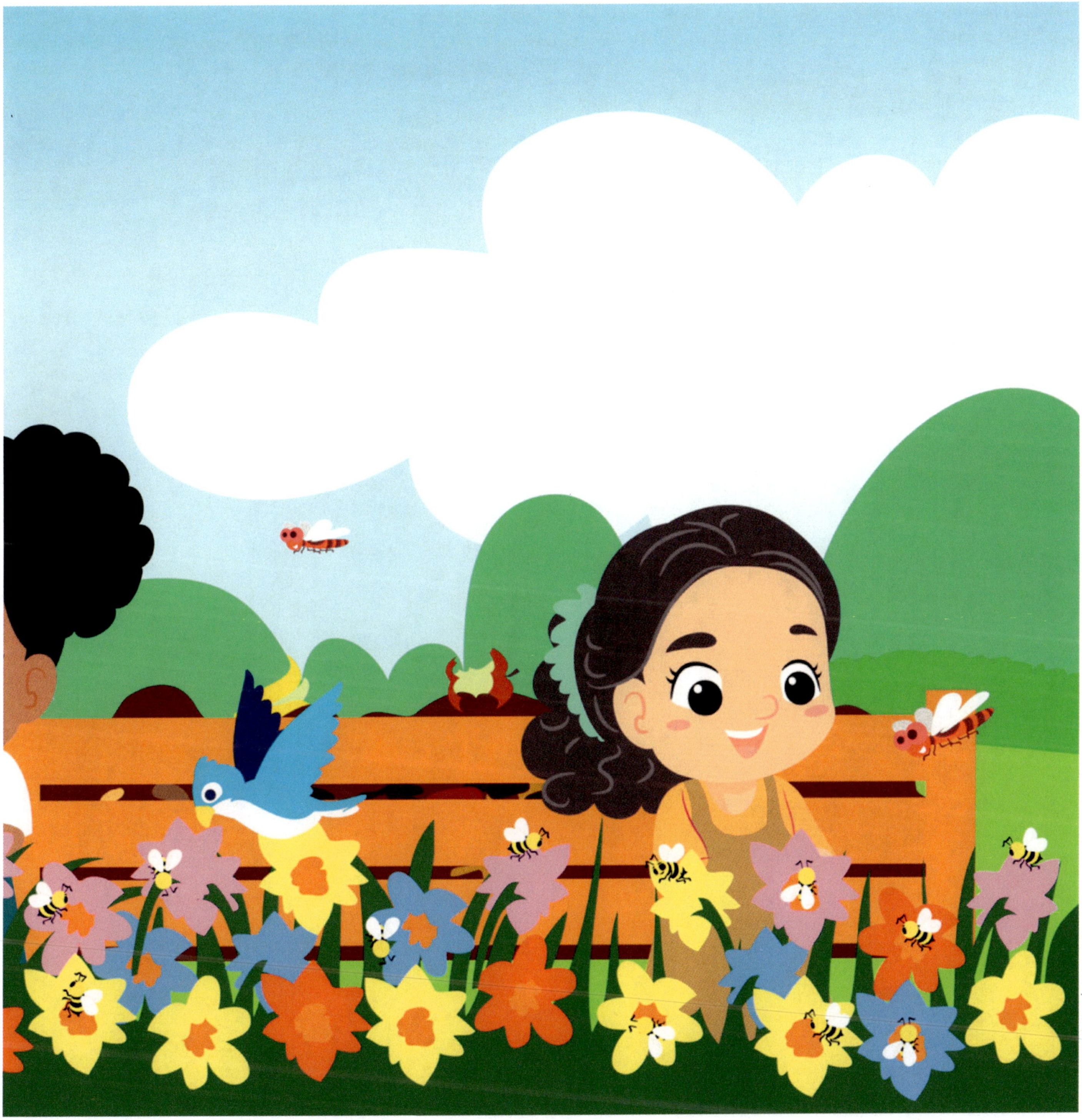

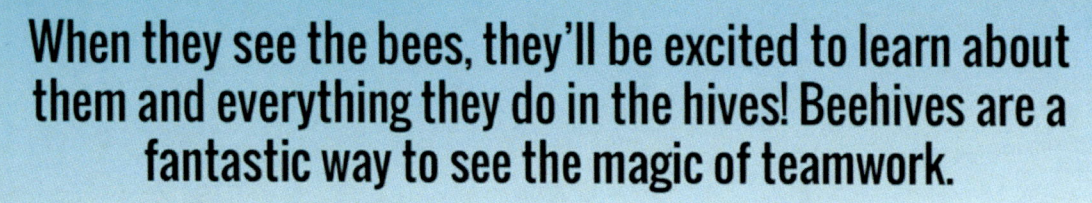

When they see the bees, they'll be excited to learn about them and everything they do in the hives! Beehives are a fantastic way to see the magic of teamwork.

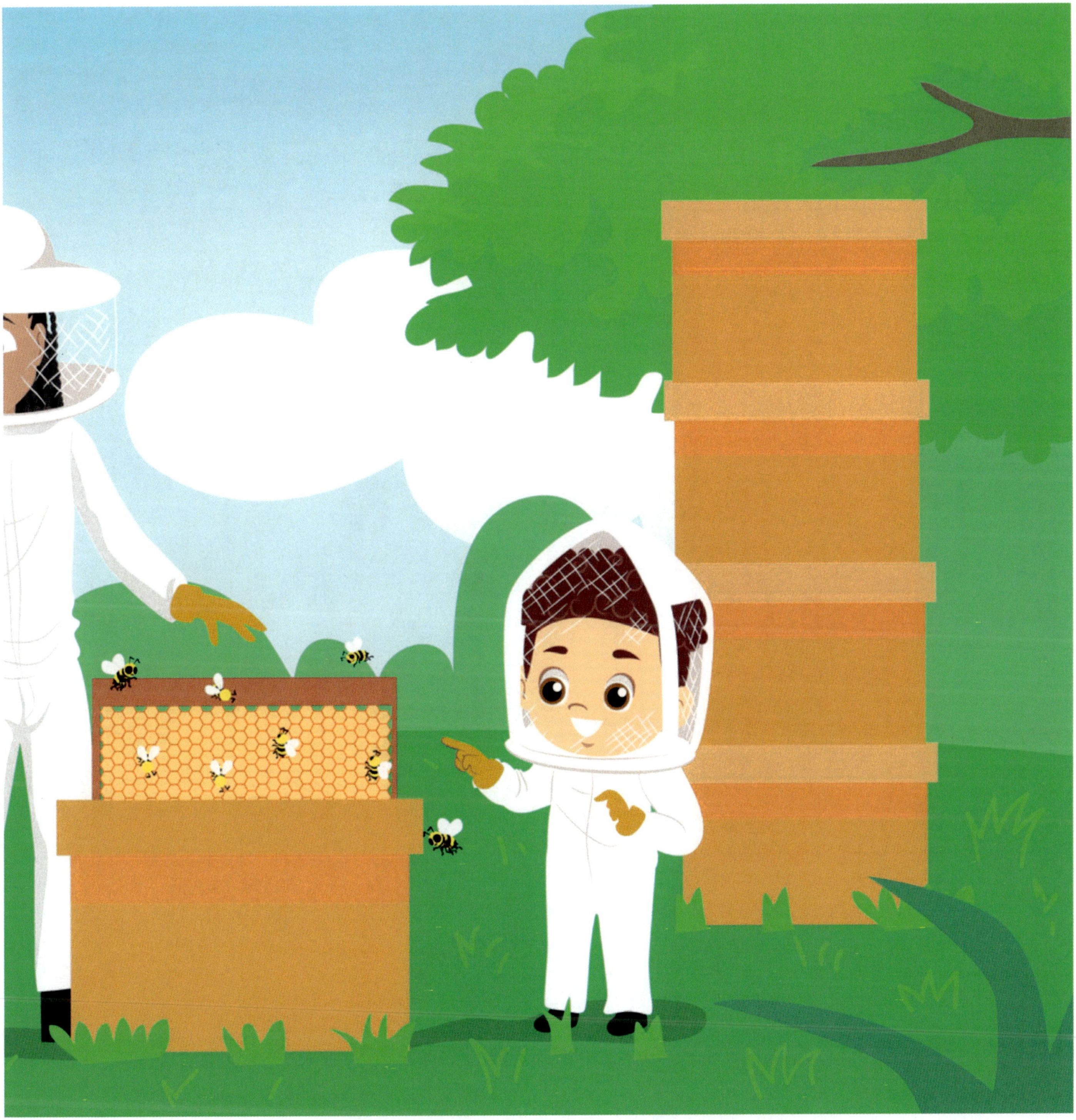

Everyone takes turns looking after the garden and the animals on the campus. At the end of each day, they'll reflect on all they've accomplished.

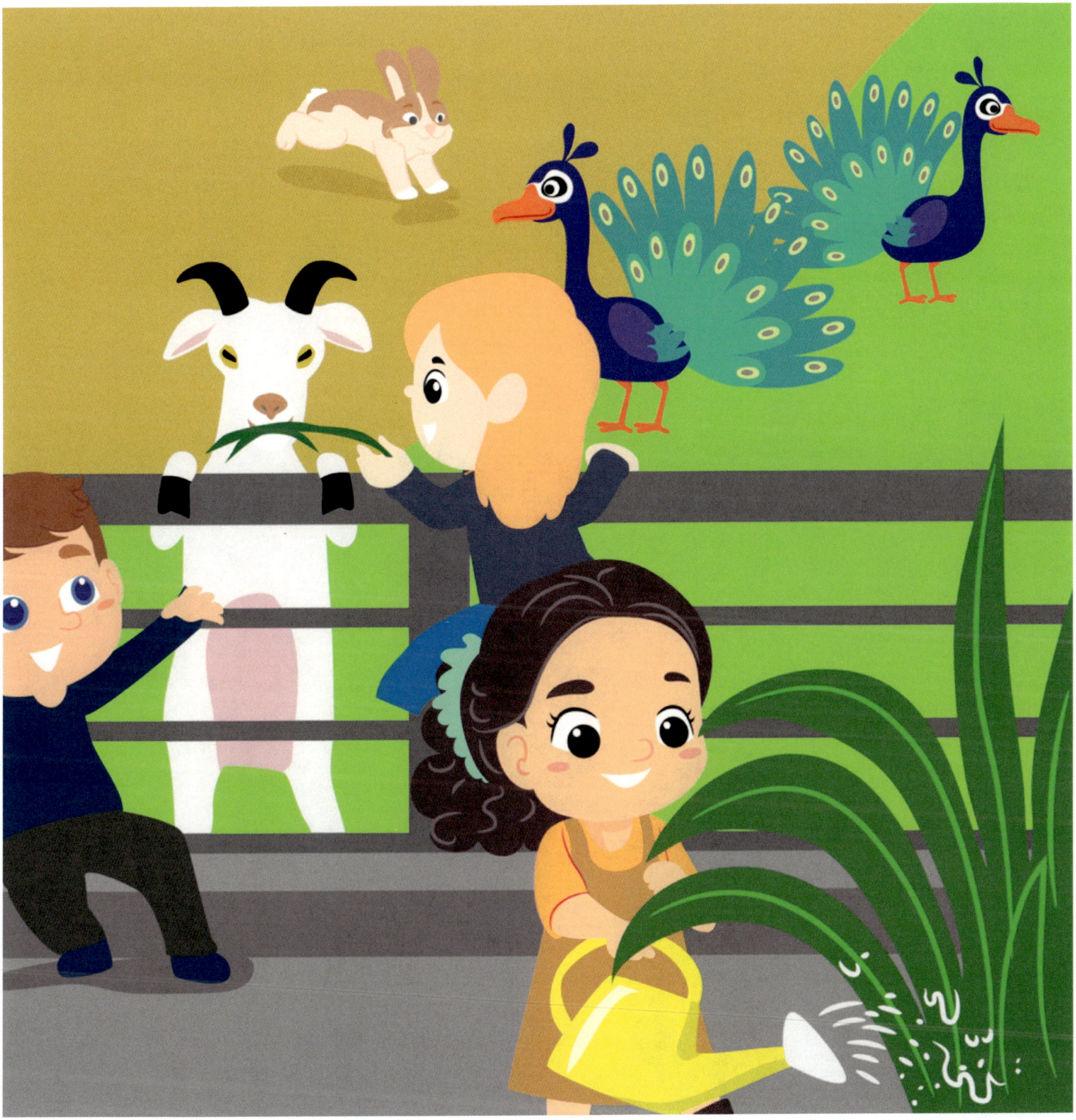

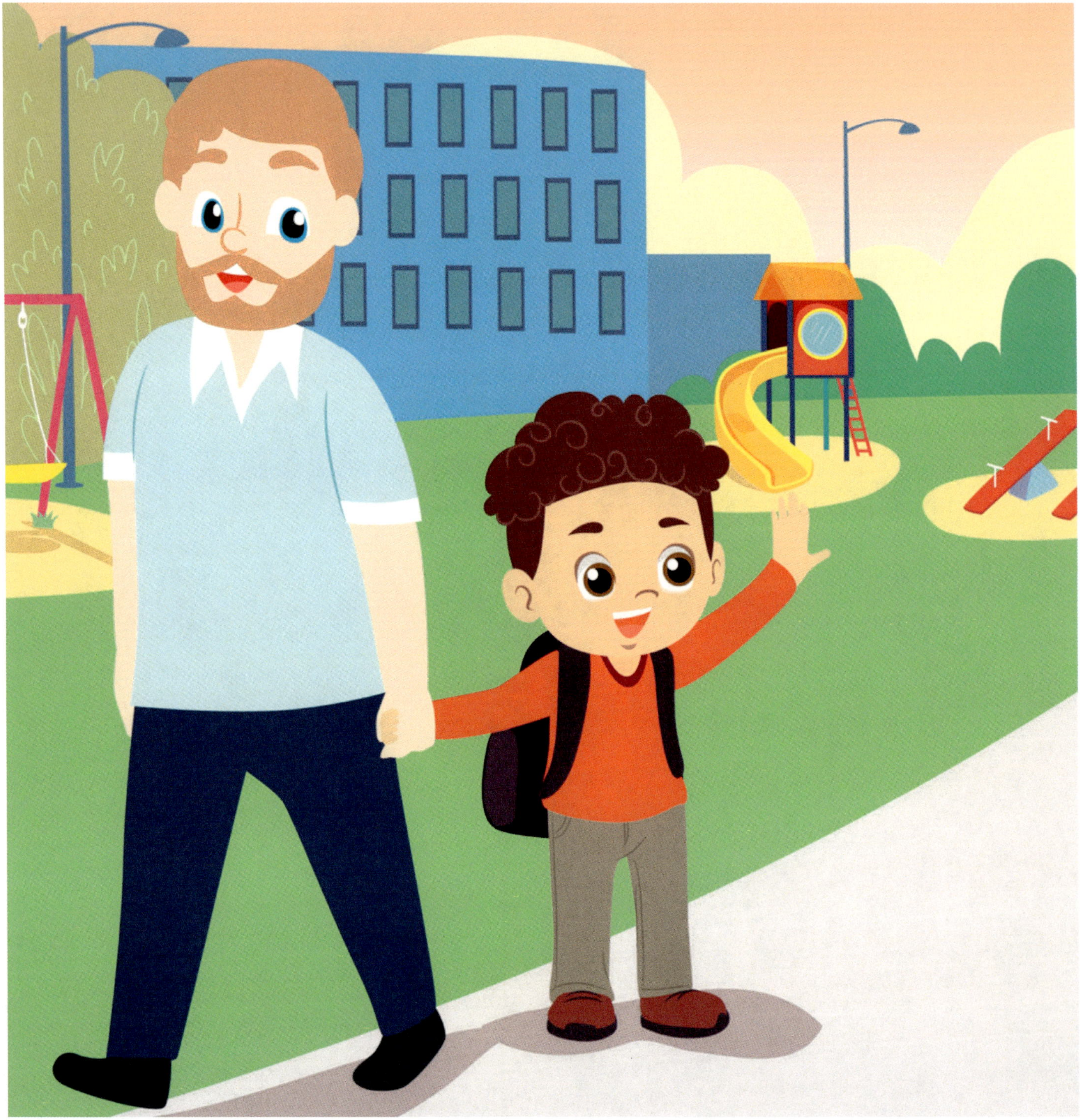

As parents arrive and they say their goodbyes, they'll eagerly await the next day, buzzing with excitement for new school adventures and discoveries waiting to be made.

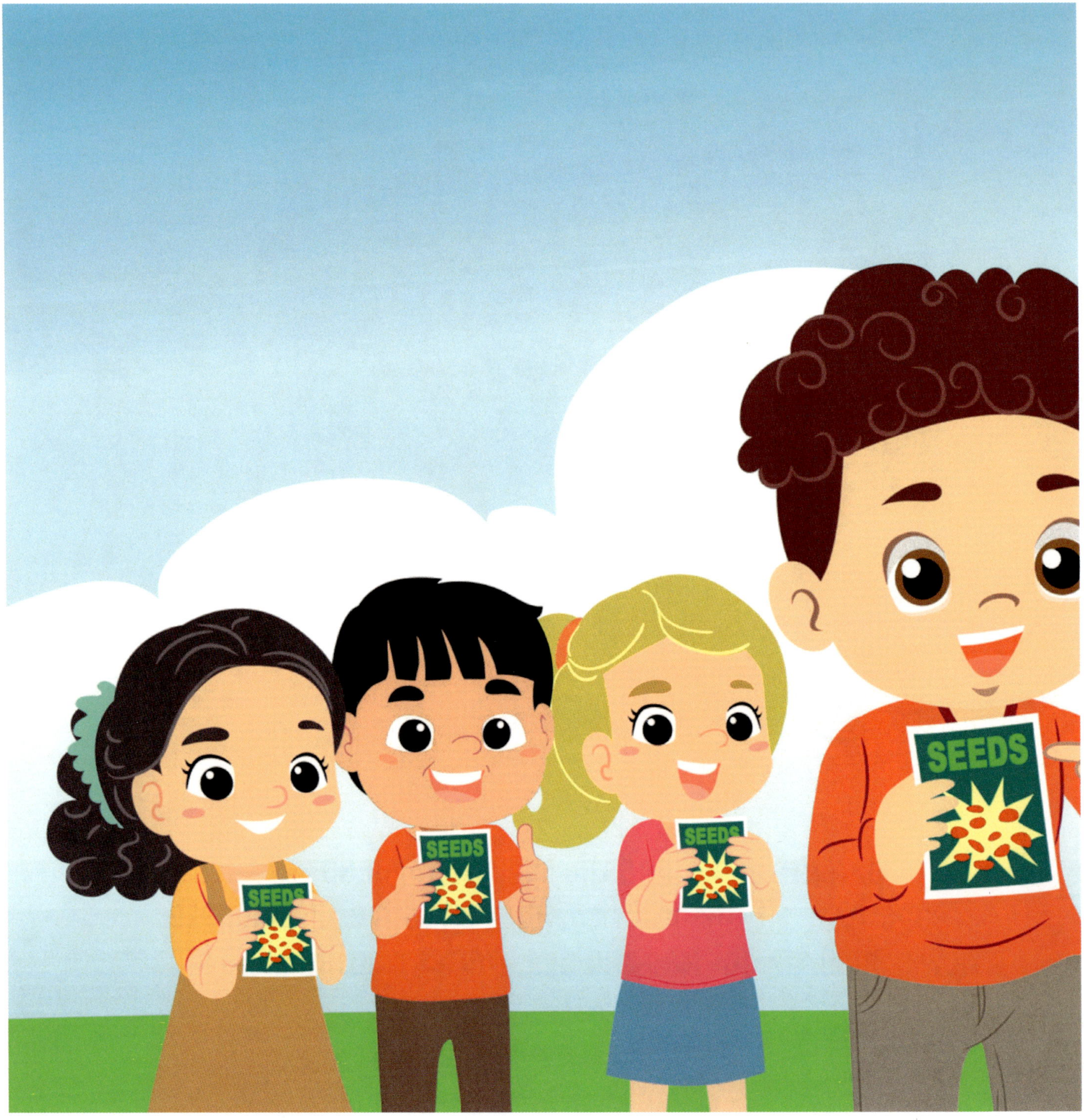
SEEDS
SEEDS
SEEDS
SEEDS

When you give a student a seed, you'll know just what they need next.
They're going to need a special place to plant it.

Made in United States
Orlando, FL
23 July 2024